Songs, Albums, & Quotes of Crosby, Stills, Nash & Young

A Pamphlet for Generation Z C.S.N.Y. Newcomers

James Curtis Geist

February 2025

BOOKS WRITTEN BY JAMES C. GEIST

I. AUTOBIOGRAPHY
MODERN AUGUSTINIAN CONFESSION:
Memoir of a Minister, Teacher & Activist
(December 2016)

II.HISTORY
The Presidents [1-45]
(February 2019)
Global History I, II, III & IV Notes for Teachers
(May 2019)
United States History Notes for Teachers
(June 2019)

III. POETRY & ANECDOTES
Bottom of the Food Chain
(June 2017)

Poetry for the Kathy Lee Gifford Child Labor Sweatshop Retirement Village
(October 2017)
A Robot Ate My Homework:
Poems & Anecdotes for the 4th Revolution Infancy
(December 2017)
Time Rich & Cash Poor
(May 2018)
Wonder Years of Teenaged Insecurity
(June 2018)
Guns & Butter, Bread & Roses
(July 2018)
Stories of the Helig, Polter & Zeitgeist
Poetry & Anecdotes *(January 2019)*
Ragbag
(March 2019)
Confession: Musings of Mischief
(April 2019)

<u>Moonquakes</u>
(February 2020)
<u>Water Wears the Stones</u>
(February 2021)
<u>Mister Fatty</u>
(May 2022)

IV.CHILDREN'S BOOKS
<u>Jimmy's Summer Beach Camping Trip</u>
(April 2018)
<u>Jimmy's Paper Route</u>
(April 2018)
<u>Jimmy's S-S-S-Summer Experience</u>
(April 2018)
<u>Jimmy's Fishing Trip</u>
(May 2019)
<u>Jimmy's Circus Trip</u>
(May 2019)
<u>Jimmy's Yard Sale</u>
(December 2020)
<u>Jimmy's Snow Day</u>
(December 2020)
<u>Jimmy's Summer Playground</u>
(December 2020)
<u>Jimmy Meets Muhammad Ali</u>
(March 2021)
<u>Jimmy's Summer Family Picnic</u>
(March 2021)

V. YOUNG ADULT
<u>Varsity Printing Team</u>
(March 2021)

VI.   COMPILATIONS
<u>Essential Geist: Volume I & II</u>
Poetry & Anecdotes   *(February 2019)*

For Bob, Rick & Gumby:

Thanks for playing

acoustic guitars late nights

in your fourth floor rooms

of Nyack College (1984-85).

They were the C.S.N.

of Moseley Hall Dorm.

TABLE OF CONTENTS

INTRODUCTION

The trademark of Crosby, Stills, Nash and Young is of vocal harmonies sounding transcendent. The years 1969-1974 were the true golden years of classical rock and rock's first supergroup merged from The Hollies, Buffalo Springfield and The Byrds. The band consisted of virtuoso musicianship and voices that were the best harmonies in music; a pure joy to listen to.

It all started with the trio's debut album that embodied what the era was about, protest songs taking on President Richard Nixon, war, love, peace and personal development. The songs "Wooden Ships", "Ohio" and "For What Its Worth" became the anthems of a generation. The vast emotional range of their music, from delicate acoustic confessionals to raucous counterculture anthems were mirrored in their personal lives as well

They were combative, volatile and songwriters who pursued chemical and female pleasured to life-threatening extremes. Over the decades, these four men would break up, reunite, disband, and get back together again. Their were musical disagreements, and self-destructive behavior in this turbulent brotherhood. This is about rock's longest-running, most dysfunctional, yet preeminent musical groups in rock history.

Rock concert promoter Bill Graham call C.S.N.Y. as the "American Beatles." The band played country rock, ballads using acoustic and electric guitars. Their second album Deja-vu sold 8 million copies.

The book includes the band's background, influences, discography and achievements. The book includes quotes and gives data why they are in the Rock and Roll Hall of Fame. This is a great book for Gen Z as an introduction to the band and music of Crosby, Stills, Nash and Young.

THE BACKGROUND OF
CROSBY, STILLS, NASH & YOUNG

1964-1966   **Band Members**

David Crosby – guitar & vocals   died in 2023
Stephen Stills – guitar & vocals
Graham Nash – guitar & vocals
Neil Young – guitar & vocals

MUSICAL INFLUENCES ON C.S.N.Y.

Folk: Stills was influenced by Folk and Latin Music.

Blues: Stills was also influenced by blues.

Jazz: Crosby was influenced by jazz and classical.

Pop: Nash was influenced by Pop.

Country: Young was influence by country and rock and
roll.

Musical Influences on Crosby, Stills, Nash and Young.

Bob Dylan	Phil Oochs
The Beatles	Jimmy Reed
The Who	Bert Jansch
Led Zeppelin	Booker T. & the M.G.s
The Rolling Stones	The Sex Pistols
Eagles	Fleetwood Mac

Short History

CSNY was born with members from three prominent
bands; Davd Crosby of The Byrds, Stephen Stills and Neil
Young from Buffalo Springfield, and Graham Nash from
The Hollies.

In 1968, Crosby, Stills and Nash experienced a pivotal moment when at dinner in Los Angeles, the three performed Stills composition, "You Don't Have to Cry" and realized their natural fluidity of their harmonies.

In 1969 they released *Crosby, Stills, Nash* with "Suite:Judy Blue Eyes," "Marrakesh Express," "Wooden Ships" and "Long Time Gone," among other hits. They signed with Atlantic Records and in 1970 released *Déjà vu* with Neil Young in the mix singing "Woodstock," "Teach Your Children Well," and "Our House."

Neil Young was to join CSN for their anticipated show at the Auditorium Theater in downtown Chicago on August 16th, 1969. There was trepidation bringing him on, for he was an immense talent, but utterly self-centered. Could they trust him at crunch time to turn up at gigs?

It was Stills idea, and Crosby was on board, but Nash was not entirely convinced. Nash agreed to meet with Young and Nash said, "Neil turned out to be a funny f__ker! I would nominate him to be prime minister of Canada. He's in. Let's give it a shot."

Nash was completely satisfied with the band's Chicago gig and the next day, they found themselves on one of the biggest stages in music history, The Woodstock Music and Arts Festival in Bethel New York.

Rolling Stone Magazine writes with Crosby's social conscious, Still's virtuoso musicianship and Nash's ability to write perfect pop melodies with voices harmonizing made their music a pure joy to listen to.

10

Influence of Laurel Canyon: 1965-1977

The Grammy Museum

The media was covering Bob Dylan in Greenwich Village
in the early 1960's and the psychedelic scene that sprung
up in San Francisco's Haight-Ashbury District a few years
later. In a few years, Laurel Canyon would be the next
wave of musical renaissance.

The band found each other amid the growing community of
Laurel Canyon in the Hollywood Hills, where housing was
cheap for poor musicians.   The three were encouraged to
work together from friends such as Joni Mitchell and
Mama Cass Elliot encouraged them to focus on their
harmonies because one plus one plus one equaled more
than three.

Laurel Canyon is not much to look at, a secluded, semi-
rural retreat for silent-movie stars. It was a quiet and
densely wooded area where a music revolution would
change the world. The likes of David Crosby and Graham
Nash worked on their music of folk-rock and country-rock
in anonymity in the 1960's and early 1970's.

Others who lived in the Canyon or frequented visiting
musical friends included members of The Byrds, The
Doors, Alan Parsons, Frank Zappa, The Turtles, Jackson
Browne, the Eagles, Joni Mitchell and Linda Ronstadt.

You could rent a house for $280 a month in 1965. The
canyon's legacy brought in the wealthy who priced out
future generations of struggling musicians. The Laurel
Canyon musicians of 1965-1977 ended up getting married,

having kids and moved downhill where the schools and birthday parties and supermarkets are.

Influence of Women on the Band

Stills developed a crush on popular folk music singer **Judy Collins** after seeing her perform in Greenwich Village in the early 1960's. Soon they were making sweet music together, meaning making whoopee. As a result, Stills wrote Suite: Judy Blue Eyes. They ended up flaming out, but Stills tried winning her back with a Martin guitar and a song he wrote about her. They two have remained friends for decades.

David Crosby and **Joni Mitchell** started dating in 1967. It was fun for Crosby, but not so much for Mitchell. She had caught David cheating with old time girlfriend **Christine Hinton** at least twice. Joni was upset and wrote a new song "That Song About the Midway" to make sure he knew how angry she really was. It was the goodbye David song.

Soon after the breakup, Mitchell hooked up with married Graham Nash. Nash fell hard for Mitchell, they lived together for several year and he was inspired to write "Our House" about their home life which eventually curdled by 1970.

Sadly in 1969, tragedy struck when Crosby's girlfriend, Christine Hinton, was killed in a car accident shortly after they moved to the Bay area. This loss pushed Crosby into deeper drug abuse, beginning a weeklong odyssey on a yacht filled with women and narcotics.

Rita Coolidge sang back up in the song "Love the One Your With." Nash set up a date with her, for he was enthralled with her. but Stills lied to her telling Coolidge Nash had changed his about meeting with her and was no longer interested. Nash was crushed when he learned about this. Coolidge eventually learned the truth, and began dating Nash. When Stills found out Rita chose Nash over him, the next time he saw Nash, *Stills came out swinging at him, but was subdued by others and pulled off him.* The relationship was stained for several years and led Nash to write the song "Frozen Smiles."

The CSNY Band Marches On

There are always yachts to be repaired, thoroughbreds to be stabled and drug habits to be funded. There are consequences with makeups such as scandals over drugs and firearms and a backstage scuffle. In the time of Vietnam-ear political protests, ecological awareness and personal growth, the band continued to meet by musical ambition. Despite it all, like a band of brothers, they continued to make music and to continue touring together.

Interesting Facts About
Crosby, Stills, Nash & Young Déjà Vu Album
Eric Alber

800 Studio Hours: Stephen Stills claims it took 800 hour to record Déjà vu, and over 100 takes for the song Déjà Vu, showcasing the perfectionism of the band.

Neil Young's Solo Contributions: Young recorded his solos in Los Angeles and sent them to the band. His contributions to "Helpless," and "Country Girl" were deeply personal.

Grief & Breakups Shaped the Mood: The album's tone came from David Crosby mourning the loss of his girlfriend Christine Hinton, while Graham Nash and Joni Mitchell and Stephen Stills and Judy Collins had ended relationships.

Joni Mitchell's "Woodstock" Transformation: Her reflective ballad became a rock anthem under Stephen Stills arrangements with the electric version added urgency and grit.

Jerry Garcia's Pedal Steel Guitar: He loaned it to CSNY for the song "Teach Your Children Well." In return, the group sang harmony for the Grateful Dead with "Workingman's Dead" and "American Beauty."

How the Band Formed: In the summer of 1968, Nash and the Hollies were invited for an evening of entertainment at Joni Mitchell's home, to hear Stills and Crosby sing. Nash was mesmerized by their performance of "You Don't Have to Cry." He asked them to sing it again, and sang with them providing harmony and the chemistry was immediate and the rest is history. Joni Mitchell unknowingly brought CSN together.

Morgan Ends – Grammys

1. **There was panic over the album cover** of the debut album, because they are not sitting in the order of Crosby, Stills, Nash, but as Nash, Stills, Crosby.

2. **CSN could have been a double album**, one acoustic,

the other electric. The final album became a blend of both.

3. **Famous friends were soaking up the sessions:**
Atlantic Records Ahmet Ertegun would show up in a limo
while Phil Spector, Cass Elliott, Judy Collins and Joni
Mitchell often turned up in the studio to watch the magic
happen.

4. **"Long Time Gone" almost did not make the album.**
Crosby wrote the song immediately after Robert F.
Kennedy was assassinated. The song meant a lot to him,
and JFK and MLK had recently been killed as well. The
song was organic and used a deeper tone as if it were a
person underwater struggling for air.

5. **Ertegun boosted their voices:** In the original mix, the
voices were relatively low. Ahment Ertegun knew the
voices were the main attraction and ordered the remix. The
band pushed back, but Ertegun signed the checks, and
thank goodness they listened to him.

C.S.N.Y DISCOGRAPHY

Studio Albums:	8
Live Albums:	6
Compilation Albums	8
Singles:	19
Video Albums:	4
Charted Songs:	7

NUMBER OF CONCERTS

CSN – 1061

CSNY – 493

STUDIO ALBUMS

1. (CSN) Crosby, Stills & Nash   [1969]

2. (CSNY) Déjà vu   [1970]

3. (CSN) CSN   [1977]

4. (CSN) Daylight Again   [1982]

5. (CSNY) American Dream   [1988]

6. (CSN) Live It Up   [1990]

7. (CSN) After the Storm   [1994]

8. (CSNY) Looking Forward   [1999]

Band Member Quotes

David Crosby

When I was in high school, I started singing in coffee
houses. My father was in the movie business, but I felt
more of an affinity and calling to singing than acting.
There are many handsome people who cannot sing

I have so much fun performing I almost feel guilty. I think,
My God, I hope no one busts me for this.

I am from a school of folk singers and the tradition of
troubadours, and you are carrying a message. . .Part of
job is to take you on a little voyage, tell you a story.

My songs emerge from my life, unbidden, unplanned and
completely on a schedule of their own.

I think music is an uplifting force, I think love is the uplifting force in the human condition. . .it rings a bell in us that elevates us. . .one of the few great things about human beings.

.I think ideas are still the most powerful things on the planet, and music is a great way to transmit them.

Sometimes the entire thing comes out in one burst. Sometimes you hack away for years before you get something that satisfies you.

Don't waste time. Time is the final currency, man. Not money, not power – it's time.

I spent a lot of time wasting talent, not treasuring it, not valuing it, not respecting it, just taking it for granted.

I don't like greed, ignorance or anger, but I love love.

I don't thing being angry is useful or healthy. When I get angry, my brain goes out the window. Boom, the adrenaline hits and instant stupid.

Being a hippy is the most natural thing to me.

I have always been a careful sailor. . .When it comes to sailing, I take it seriously and take spares of everything. You have to be careful, because when you are 1500 miles from land, there is no one you can call. You are on your own.

Good music is an end in itself. . .it's really the most fun.

CSN is like juggling four bottles of nitroglycerine.

Stephen Stills

Once you decide that it is the art that is important and not
how popular and well received you are, you no longer
have an albatross.

One thing the blues ain't is funny.

If you can't be with the one you love, love the one
your're with.

There are three things me can do with women: love them,
suffer for them, or turn them into literature.

Sometimes I get a little drunk, a little out of it, or my guitar
gets out of tune onstage, but that is something that
should not get dissected.

I much prefer the road. My thing is getting live on stage in
front of people. The studio environment is sterile to
me.

David (Crosby) knows everyone – he is a social butterfly.

I moved around so much as a kid, the place I call home is
New Orleans because I can remember the names of
some of the streets there.

I spent my last year of high school in Latin America, and
there's an edge of salsa under all of my rhythms.

I got hooked into folk music by accident, because that is
white college kids liked when I was a child.

I don't set out to write a political song. I just write about
what is going on.

Graham Nash

There is a great correlation between music and images.

Being in a different band [Nash – Hollies; Stills/Young – Buffalo Springfield; Crosby – The Byrds] always brings musical experiences to draw on.

There are always new things to experience, internalize and then write about. This process is ongoing and never stops.

If I read or listened to music critics of our music, I'd have been discouraged a long time ago.

Martin guitars came out with a Stephen Stills model and it is beautiful I bought one immediately.

I think Stephen Stills is playing better than ever.

After six or seven performances of any song, you begin to perform it instead of feeling it.

When I was born in 1942 (England), World War II was still going on. I realized if we don't teach our kids a better way of relating to their fellow human beings, the future of humanity on the planet is in jeopardy.

I am still hear and alive and every year has been fantastic.

Neil's (Young) effect on the band was immediate and very fulfilling. He adds edge and is an incredible musician. We became a better band because of him.

Neil Young

The 60's was the first time the power of music was used by a generation to bind them together.

I do what I do. I like to make music.

There is an edge to rock and roll. It's all that matters.

One new feature or fresh take can change everything.

I live for playing live. All my records are live since *After the Gold Rush. . .*

I don't think I'm a thorn in the side of industry, I am just part of it.

I don't like war. I particularly do not like the celebration of war.

I'm not into organized religion. I believe in a higher source of creation, and we are all just part of nature.

As I get older, I get smaller. . .I see outside myself more.

I could be likened to an old hound circling on a rug for the last five years.

Some CSNY Song Lyrics

Ohio Neil Young
Tin soldiers and Nixon coming,
We're finally on our own.
This summer I hear the drumming,
Four dead in Ohio.

Suite: Judy Blue Eyes   Stephen Stills
It's getting to the point, where I am no fun anymore,
I am sorry.
Sometimes it hurst so badly, I must cry,
I am lonely.
I am yours, you are mine, you are what you are.
You make it hard.

Marrakesh Express   Graham Nash
Sweeping cobwebs from the edges of my mind
Had to get away to see what we could find.
Hope the days that lie ahead
Bring us back to where they's led.

Wouldn't you know we're riding
on the Marrakesh Express? (2x)
They are taking me to Marrakesh.
All aboard the train.

Guinnevere   David Crosby
Guinnevere had green eyes
Like yours, mi'lady, like yours.
When she'd walk down through the garden
In the morning after it rained
Peacocks wandered aimlessly
Underneath an orange tree
Why can't she see me?

Wooden Ships   Crosby, Stills & Paul Kanter
Wooden ships on the water, very free & easy.
Easy, you know, the way it's supposed to be.
Silver people on the shoreline, let us be,
Talkin' about free and easy.

21

Horror grips us as we watch you die.
All we can do is echo your anguished cries.
Stare as all human feelings die.
We are leaving, so you don't need us.

Lady of the Island   Graham Nash
Holding you close undisturbed before the fire,
The pressure in my chest when you breathe in my ear.
We both knew this would happen when you first appeared,
My lady of the island.

Helplessly Hoping   Stephen Stills
Helplessly hoping her harlequin hovers nearby,
Awaiting a word.
Gasping at glimpses of gentle true spirit, he runs,
Wishing he could fly.
Only to trip at the sound of goodbye.

Cathedral   Graham Nash
I'm flying in Winchester Cathedral
Sunlight pouring through the break of day.
Stumbled though the door and into the chamber…
And feeling deep inside of me

Tells me this place can be the place…
I'm flying Winchester Cathedral.
All religion has to have its day
Expressions on the face of the Savior
Made me say I can't stay…

Teach Your Children Well   Graham Nash
You, who are on the road, must have a code

That you can live by.
And so, become yourself, because the past
is just a goodbye.
Teach, your children well…
Feed them on your dreams…
Look and sigh and know they love you.

Helpless   Neil Young
There is a town in north Ontario
With dream comfort and memory to spare
And in my mind I need a place to go.
All my changes were there.

Blue, blue windows behind the stars,
Yellow moon on the rise.
Big birds flying across the sky,
Throwing shadows on our eyes.

Just a Song Before I Go   Graham Nash
Just a song before I go, to whom it may concern.
Traveling twice the speed of sound it's easy to get burned.

Our House   Graham Nash
Our house is a very, very, very fine house.
With two cats in the yard,
life used to be so hard,
now everything is easy 'cause of you.'

Daylight Again   Graham Nash
There's so much time to make up, everywhere you turn…
So much water moving underneath the bridge.
Let the water come and carry us away.

Meanings of Some of the Song Lyrics

Marrakesh Express: (Graham Nash)
In 1966 I read a book on the Beat Poets and went to Marrakesh and all they did was smoke dop and write. I took a trip on a train, was bored on first class and went to third class and saw real life. I went back to first class to write the song.

Cathedral: (Graham Nash)
This was born from a realization most of the world's wars in most part, are created from religious differences. This song was a real experience when I took LSD and laid in the middle of the Stonehenge Stones.

Immigration Man: (Graham Nash)
The song came out of anger. I was in Vancouver with CSNY, and at the border, I could not get in because I was on a H-1 visa from England. I was not American, I was giving autographs, and when I got back to San Francisco, I wrote the song.

Wind on the Water: (Crosby & Nash)
In England, Crosby was hated by the press. He was the great whale with harpoons being thrown. . .When CSN first broke up, Crosby took me out on his 60 foot sailing yacht. A 90 foot whale came within 50 feet of us with a dozen dolphins swimming around. This is where the song came from.

Our House: (Graham Nash)
A love song for Joni Mitchell in one sense, and for every woman in another sense.

Helplessly Hoping: (Stephen Stills)
Inspired by my 10th grade English teacher in Tampa Florida. She was a knockout, and was able to get football players to read poetry in class. I tried to impress her with awful poetry I wrote. I guess some of it rubbed off on me.

Ohio: (Neil Young)
It was penned as a direct result of the National Guard shooting and killing four Kent State college students protesting the Vietnam War on May 4th, 1970.

Carry On: (Stephen Stills)
Almost sounding like two songs bridged by "Carry on...Love is coming to us all." It was a generational pleas and a call to arms for themselves struggling with band cohesion.

Almost Cut My Hair: (David Crosby)
Adopted as the countercultural generation or hippies that did not conform to society's standards. Let your freak flags fly!

Wooden Ships: (Crosby, Stills, Katner)
It is about ship wrecked survivors of opposing war sides having to create a new civilization to survive.

Southern Cross: (Stephen Stills)
With the countercultural movement done, CSN still created in the 1980s. After a painful divorce, Stills writes about the fabled constellations stars, and about using the power of the universe to heal your wounds.

C.S.N.Y and C.S.N. ALBUMS
RATED BY SALES

1. **DÉJÀ VU** (1970) **[CSNY]**
   Sales: 7,966,100

2. **CROSBY, STILLS, NASH** (1969)
   Sales: 4,270,000

3. **CSN** (1977)
   Sales: 4,010,690

4. **AMERICAN DREAM** (1988) **[CSNY]**
   Sales: 1,000,000

5. **DAYLIGHT AGAIN** (1982)
   Sales: 1,160,001

6. **LOOKING FORWARD** (1999) **[CSNY]**
   Sales: 400,000

7. **LIVE IT UP** (1969)
   Sales: 300,000

8. **AFTER THE STORM** (1994)
   Sales: 200,000

C.S.N.'s EIGHT STUDIO ALBUMS

1. Crosby, Stills, Nash (1969)

a. Suite: Judy Blue Eyes
b. Marrakesh Express
c. Guinnevere
d. You Don't Have to Cry
e. Pre Road Downs
h. Wooden Ships
i. Lady of the Island
j. Helplessly Hoping
k. Long Time Gone
l. 49 Bye-Byes

26

2. <u>Déjà Vu</u> (1970)

a. Carry On
b. Teach Your Children
c. Almost Cut My Hair
d. Helpless
e. Woodstock
f. Deja Vu
g. Our House

h. 4 + 20
i. Country Girl
2. Whiskey Boot Hill
2. Down, Down, Down
3. I Think U R Pretty
k. Everybody I Love You

3. <u>CSN</u> (1977)

a. Shadow Captain
b. See the Changes
c. Carried Away
d. Fair Game
e. Anything at All
f. Cathedral

g. Dark Star
h. Just a Song Before I Go
i. Run from Tears
j. Cold Rain
k. In My Dreams
l. I Give You Give Blind

4. <u>Daylight Again</u> (1982)

a. Turn Your Back on Love
b. Wasted on the Way
c. Southern Cross
d. Into the Darkness
e. Delta
f. Since I Met You

g. Too Much Love to Hide
h. Song for Susan
i. You Are Alive
j. Might as Well Have a
   Good Time
k. Daylight Again/Find the
   Cost of Freedom

5. American Dream (1988)

a. American Dream
b. Got It Made
c. Name of Love
d. Don't Say Goodbye
e. This Old House
f. Nighttime for the Generals
g. Shadowland
g. Drivin' Thunder
h. Clear Blue Skies
i. That Girl
j. Compass
k. Soldier of Peace
l. Feel Your Love
m. Night Song

6. Live It Up (1990)

a. Live It Up
b. If Anybody Had a Heart
c. Tomboy
d. Haven't We Lost Enough
e. Yours & Mine
f. (Got to Keep) Open
g. Straight Line
h. House of Broken Dreams
i. Arrows
j. After the Dolphin

7. After the Storm (1994)

a. Only Waiting for You
b. Find a Dream
c. Camera
d. Unequal Love
e. Till It Shines
f. It Won't Go Away
g. These Empty Days
h. In My Life
i. Street to Lean On
j. Bad Boyz
k. After the Storm
l. Panama

8. Looking Forward (1999)

a. Faith in Me
b. Looking Forward
c. Stand & Be Counted
d. Heartland
e. Seen Enough
f. Slowpoke
g. Dream for Him
h. No Tears Left
i. Out of Control
j. Someday Soon
k. Queen of Them All
l. Sanibel

Singles of CSNY/CSN
Top Ten Songs - (VCR Music)

1. Suite: Judy Blue Eyes
2. Ohio
3. Helpless
4. Woodstock
5. Carry On
6. Long Time Ago
7. Our House
8. Teach Your Children
9. Just a Song Before I Go
10. Marrakesh Express

CSN Songs 15 Greatest Songs Ranked
Gold Radio – Thomas Curtis-Horsfall

1. Our House
2. Suite: Judy Blue Eyes
3. Woodstock
4. Ohio
5. Helplessly Hoping
6. Carry On
7. Almost Cut My Hair
8. Helpless
9. Marrakesh Express
10. Long Time Ago
11. Teach Your Children
12. Turn Your Back on Love
13. Just a Song Before I Go
14. Southern Cross
15. Wooden Ships

Billboard's Top 100 CSNY /CSN Songs

7.   Just a Song Before I Go (5-28-77)
9.   Wasted on the Way (6-6-82)
18. Southern Cross (9-18-82)
21. Suite: Judy Blue Eyes (10-4-69)
28. Marrakesh Express (7-19-69)
43. Fair Game (10-1-71)
45. War Games (6-25-83)
69. Too Much Love to Hide (1-29-83)

Possible Combinations of CSNY

Crosby, Stills, Nash, Young,	***No Combos Yet***
Crosby, Stills, Nash	Crosby, Stills, Young
Crosby/Nash	Crosby, Nash, Young
Stills/Young	Stills, Nash, Young
Crosby	Crosby/Young
Stills	Crosby/Stills
Nash	Nash/Young
Young	Nash/Stills

Albums by Crosby/Nash

Graham Nash David Crosby	1972
Wind on the Water	1975
Whistling down the Wire	1976
Crosby & Nash	2004

Albums by Stills/Young (Buffalo Springfield)

Buffalo Springfield	1966
Buffalo Springfield Again	1967
Last Time Around	1968

Stills-Young Band

Long May You Run	1976

Graham Nash (The Hollies)

Stay with the Hollies	1964
In the Hollies Style	1964
Hollies	1965
Would You Believe	1966
Bus Stop	1966
For Certain Because	1966
Evolution	1967
Butterfly	1967

Albums by David Crosby

If I Could Remember My Name	1971
Oh Yes I Can	1989
Thousand Roads	1993
Croz	2014
Lighthouse	2016
Sky Trails	2017
Here If You Listen	2018
For Free	2021

Albums by Stephen Stills

Super Session	1968	
Stephen Stills	1970	
Stephen Stills 2	1971	
Manassas	1972	
Down the Road	1973	
Stills	1975	
Stephen Stills Live	1975	
Illegal Stills	1976	
Best of Stephen Stills	1976	
Thoroughfare Gap	1978	
Right by You	1984	
Stills Alone	1991	
Turnin' Back the Pages	2003	
Man Alive!	2005	
Pieces	2009	
Carry On	2013	
Can't Get Enough	2013	(The Rides)
Pierced Arrow	2016	
Everybody Knows	2017	(with Judy Collins)
Live at Berkely	2023	(recorded in 1971)

Albums by Graham Nash

Songs for Beginners	1971
Wild Tales	1974
Earth & Sky	1980
Innocent Eyes	1986
Songs for Survivors	2002
This Path Tonight	2016
Now	2023

Albums by Neil Young

Neil Young	1968	
Everybody Knows This is Nowhere	1969	(w Crazy Horse)
After the Gold Rush	1970	
Harvest	1972	
On the Beach	1974	
Tonight's the Night	1975	
Zuma	1975	(w Crazy Horse)
Long May You Run	1976	
Comes a Time	1978	
Rust Never Sleeps	1979	(w Crazy Horse)
Hawks & Doves	1980	
Reactor	1981	(w Crazy Horse)
Trans	1982	
Everybody's Rockin'	1983	(w the Shocking Pinks)
Old Ways	1985	
Landing on Water	1986	
Life	1987	(w Crazy Horse)
This Note's for You	1988	(w The Blue Notes)
Freedom	1989	

Ragged Glory	1990	(w Crazy Horse)
Harvest Moon	1992	
Sleeps with Angels	1994	(w Crazy Horse)
Mirror Ball	1995	(w Pearl Jam)
Broken Arrow	1996	(w Crazy Horse)
Silver & Gold	2000	
Are You Passionate?	2002	(w Booker T & the M.G.s)
Greendale	2003	(w Crazy Horse)
Prairie World	2005	
Living with War	2006	
Fork in the Road	2009	
Le Noise	2010	
Americana	2012	(w Crazy Horse)
Psychedelic Pill	2012	(w Crazy Horse)
A Letter Home	2014	
Storytime	2014	
The Monsanto Years	2015	(w Promise of the Real)
Peace Trail	2016	
The Visitor	2017	(w Promise of the Real)
Colorado	2019	(w Crazy Horse)
Barn	2021	(w Crazy Horse)
World Record	2022	

The voices of David Crosby, Stephen Stills and Graham Nash have helped define history through music. Crosby Stills and Nash became of the most influential acts in music history through their song writing genius, stunning harmonies and political activism. Before Neil Young joined, the foursome had time to grow as artists with other bands to help create the first Supergroup in the Rock world. **-Cillea Houghton**

Achievements

Created 8 studio albums, 6 live & 8 compilation
   albums.

1970: Grammy - Best New Artist of the Year

1970: Déjà vu Number 1 album

1970: Grammy - Best Vocals Performance by a
   group.

1971: Four Way Street – Number 1 Album

1974: So Far – Compilation Album certified
   platinum 6 x.

1978: Best Pop Vocal Performance by a Group for
   CSN

1997: Inducted into the Hall of Fame CSN/CSNY

The quartet has sold 20 million albums,
   the trio has sold 13 million albums
   the combined quartet, trio, duos and solos
      combined have sold 70 million albums.

Have seven top hit singles on Billboard's Top 100.

Printed in Dunstable, United Kingdom